BREA THE

Over 100 innovative ice-breakers

Pete Townsend

Kevin
Mayhew

First published in 2001 by
KEVIN MAYHEW LTD
Buxhall, Stowmarket
Suffolk IP14 3BW
Email: info@kevinmayhewltd.com

The material in this book first appeared in *Café Logos Year A*, *Martha's Diner* and *Martha's Diner 2*.

9 8 7 6 5 4 3 2 1 0

ISBN 1 84003 835 7
Catalogue No. 1500463

Cover design by Angela Selfe
Edited and typeset by Elisabeth Bates

Printed and bound in Great Britain

Contents

Acknowledgements	5
Introduction	7
General starters	9
Acceptance	16
Ambition	19
Anger	21
Authority	23
Baptism	25
Christian life	27
Confidence	35
Death	38
Decisions	40
Doubt	46
Faith	49
Fear	51
Forgiveness	54
Freedom	56
Friendship	57
Gossip	58
Honesty	59
Love	64
Love of God	65

CONTENTS

Perseverance	67
Problems	69
Self-image	71
Serving God	78
Social justice	79
Time	82
Trust	83
Worry	92
Worship	94

Acknowledgements _____

Often, when you look back at what went on before, you wonder how you got to be where you are right now. I wouldn't like to go back to many of the hassles that I somehow got tangled up with, but I would really like to thank those who frequently, and without reservation, gave me a hand out of the pit.

Thanks Billy & Co for the listening ear and copious amounts of encouragement. To Ed and Jane who always come to the rescue with grape juice. To Liz for being there and to Dave for remaining wacky. Most of all to my wife Ruth, for every moment of every day together.

Introduction

How many hours have you spent wondering how to introduce a topic that has all the potential of becoming the biggest yawn since documentaries were invented? Have you calculated how many mugs of tea have gone cold while you've waited for that vital spark of inspiration to ignite your grey cells? Have you ever looked on in sheer amazement at the ability of an audience to lurch into slumber while you've sweated your way through two sentences of introduction? If you've been there then this book might just help you survive those initial embarrassing moments when everyone, including yourself, wonders what you're going on about.

If you're looking for safe, tub-thumping, high-gloss ice-breakers then you might find some of the enclosed ideas a little off the beaten track. The following ice-breakers have a certain 'light the blue touchpaper and see what happens' approach. Many of the ideas here are intended to surprise and rattle a few brain cells.

The most important thing is that you and everybody else have fun getting to grips with topics that can tend to run aground on the rocks of adolescent indifference. More importantly, it's vital to get everyone feeling as though they are totally involved in the proceedings. Giving people a sense of belonging is great. Giving people something to think about is brilliant. Giving them something to laugh about is awesome.

Before you start, consider a few points:

- The old Scout motto, 'Be prepared'. Think through the ice-breaker first. Make sure that you have all the equipment ready and, above all, read through the instructions until you are confident that you can achieve the desired result.

- If you're not willing to get totally involved and possibly make a fool of yourself, then nobody else will.

- Never push anyone beyond their capability or into doing something that will make them feel uncomfortable. Be sensitive to each individual.

- Be honest with yourself and with the group. Forget about trying to appear 'cool'; give the group somebody to laugh at!

- Don't come across as someone who has all the answers. You can learn just as much from the group as they can from you.

- Get to know your group. Be aware of each individual's character and their circumstances.

- Be flexible. Some things may not work with the dynamics of the group. Always have some alternative ideas available.

- Have fun!

General starters

1

Equipment: large sheets of paper and a marker pen

Tell the group that although you know the topic for today's session you thought that it would make a change if they had to work out the topic by playing hangman. Allow each member of the group three guesses. (Either allow each member three guesses only or deduct one guess every time a wrong guess is made.) Once they have run out of guesses they cannot take any further part in the game.

2

Equipment: postcards (sufficient for most members of the group to take part in the game)

Each of the cards should have a word on but with a variety of definitions. This is a type of biblical *Call My Bluff*. For example:

BAMAH

Definition 1: During Old Testament times people who were unfortunate enough to find themselves homeless could go to a small community where they would be looked after and provided with basic accommodation. The word *Bamah* refers to a kind of supervisor or manager of the community who would be in charge of all the people who cared for the temporary residents.

Definition 2: In the Hebrew language there are some words which have a very general meaning. The word *Bamah* simply means a high place. So, rather than say 'on top of a tall building', or 'a mountain peak', the word *Bamah* is used. (Correct definition.)

SACKBUT

Definition 1: A *sackbut* is, in fact, a type of musical instrument. It's a kind of early trombone which was used during Old Testament times.
(Correct definition.)

Definition 2: A *sackbut* was an early form of washing basket. It wasn't used for domestic clothes but for storing the sacks that grain and herbs were kept in. After you had emptied a sack of grain or herbs, you would place the dirty sack in the *sackbut* to be washed, ready for re-use.

You can write more cards and make up definitions by using a Bible dictionary and a little zany imagination. Divide the group into teams and give each team a selection of words. Each player reads out a definition and the other team have to decide which is the correct definition.

3

Equipment: cards, or sheets of paper with parts of headlines written in large letters
pens and paper

Distribute the cards to each member of the group. (Some members may have more than one card.) Divide the group into twos or threes. Ask each group to try and make 'head-lines' using the words on their cards. Can anyone make up a story to match the headline?

Headline words:

One man	Purple shoes	for	the
Toffee ice-cream	Mild explosion	and	an
Escaped budgie	in	today	
Last night	Runs around	with	
Toothless monkey	yesterday	next	
Hours	Rubber bucket	of	
Attempts to fly	in	a	

4

Equipment: large cards or A4 sheets

Take ten cards and write the following headlines:

'Budgie eats tube of Smarties!'
'Sales of coloured tissues drop'
'Two injured in ice-cream fight!'
'Forty witnesses to chocolate bar theft'
'Lorry carrying paint overturns. Multicoloured motorway'
'Police fear local car thief may strike again'
'Government declare national holiday every Monday'
'Island disappears after volcanic eruption'
'United Nations calls for world-wide nuclear testing ban'
'Local man swallows Guinness book of records!'

Show each headline to the group. For each headline ask the group whether it should be reported in the local newspaper or national newspaper; on local radio or national radio; local TV or national TV?

5

Equipment: sticky labels

Before the group arrive write the following words onto the sticky labels:

Pebble	Boulder	Tree	Raspberry
Bush	Twig	Lemon	Banana
Carrot	Potato	Lettuce	Onion
Jam	Butter	Honey	Salt

You can add more items to suit the number of the group. As the group arrive stick one of the labels on their backs, but don't tell them what it is. Tell everyone to move around and ask other members of the group, 'What is my item?' The other group members have to mime the item and can only answer yes or no to questions. When someone has guessed

11

correctly what their item is they can sit down and watch the others trying to guess theirs.

6

Equipment: cards

Prepare the cards by writing one of the following words on each one:

straight	tall	ugly	hard	narrow
small	wide	deep	wet	dry
shallow	beautiful	twisted	dark	
light	open	shut	soft	

Divide the group into two teams. Shuffle the cards. One team member from Group A selects a card and mimes the word on the card to their group. The rest of Group A try to guess the mime but, to win a point, they must answer with the opposite of the mimed word! If they answer with the mimed word they lose a point. If they cannot guess, the other group are allowed to guess. The teams take it in turns to guess the opposite of the mimed word and score or lose points accordingly.

7

Equipment: pack of playing cards

Select sufficient cards for each member of the group to have *one* card. Make sure you include either the Queen of Clubs or the Queen of Spades, but not both. Shuffle the cards and distribute one card to each member of the group. The group must not show their card to any other member of the group. The game is simple. The holder of the black queen has to eliminate the other members of the group by winking at them once. The person winked at counts to ten, then places their card in front of them and says 'I'm out'. They must not identify the person who winked at them. If a member of the group thinks they know who's 'winking' then they are allowed to accuse them. If they are wrong, the accuser is out of the game. The game continues until everyone is 'out' or the eliminator is discovered.

8

Equipment: flipchart
glue or tacks
assorted pictures
pens and paper

Select a variety of pictures taken from a wide range of magazines and/or newspapers. Cut out a portion of the picture so that the image is incomplete (remember to keep a note of what the picture was originally). Stick/glue the images onto the flipchart and number each image.

Distribute the pens and paper to the group and ask them to guess what the original picture was. The person with the most correct answers is the winner.

9

Equipment: card/flipchart
paper
pens

Listed below are all the major planets of our own sun. Firstly, the planets' names have been rearranged and, secondly, they are not in order according to distance. Have the list displayed on card or a flipchart. Each group member needs to unravel the planet's name and then list them in order of distance beginning with the nearest to the sun and furthest away from the sun.

1. Heart	4. Nuves	7. Teen pun
2. Rams	5. Nutars	8. Tierupj
3. Curry me	6. Lutop	9. Suruna

The correct order should be Mercury, Venus, Earth, Mars, Jupiter, Saturn. Uranus, Neptune, Pluto.

Distribute the paper and pens to the group and ask them to solve the planetary problem!

10

Equipment: postcard for each member of the group

On each postcard write *one* letter and *one* word, which begins with the same letter of the alphabet. Either allow each group member to select a card at random (have the cards face down), or tape a card under each seat. If the group is fairly small, simply ask them to get their cards and try to make as many words as possible. This is done in the following way. Firstly, the group should look at their combined words and see what sort of sentence they can make using the words only (not all of the cards have to be used). They may not be able to make a complete, or sensible, sentence with the words they've got. This is where the single letters come into play. Once the group have decided on a sentence, they can then see what word/s they can make from the letters, which can then be included in the sentence.

If the group is large enough, give each member of the group a number. Call out a sequence of random numbers and those members must try and form a sentence using their words and letters.

There are some variations of the above game. You can ask the group to firstly make a word using the letters and then combine this word into a sentence that is made with the other words on the cards. Alternatively, have the words on one set of cards and the single letters on another set. Give out the words first and ask the group to make a sentence. Then give out the single letter cards and make a word from these letters. Once they have done this ask the group to include the new word in the sentence which they have previously made.

11

Equipment: postcards
blindfolds
chairs

Write one of the following instructions onto each postcard.

Turn left one step
Turn right one step
Go forward one step
Go backwards one step
Go forward two steps
Go backwards two steps

Have several copies of each instruction. Invite one member of the group to be blindfolded. Stand them in the centre of the room. Place a number of chairs around the room randomly. Shuffle the cards and ask one member of the group to take one card and read it aloud. The blindfolded member of the group must do exactly what the card tells them to do. Invite a second member of the group to pick another card and read it, again the blindfolded member follows the instructions.

Repeat the process until all the cards are used up or the blindfolded member cannot go any further. If the group member reaches a wall or door, take another card until one of them gives an opportunity to move away from the obstacle.

You can make this game more fun/difficult by having two or three blindfolded members starting at different points of the room, each responding to the same card.

Acceptance

1

Equipment: tube of 'Smarties' or similar sweets

As the group arrive, select two or three members to sit alone in a corner of the room, well away from the other members of the group. Ask the remaining group members to ignore the two or three members sitting on their own. Sit close to the rest of the group and ask them what kind of week they have had, and what interesting things have happened to them. While you are talking, begin to share the sweets with these group members. (Keep some sweets for the two or three 'outsiders', but don't make this known.)

After a few minutes gather all the group together and ask the 'outsiders' what they were thinking while the rest of the group were talking and eating sweets together. Ask the rest of the group how they felt about the group members who were 'left out' of things? Did the 'outsiders' feel rejected? Feel amused? Did they feel they had done something wrong?

2

Equipment: postcard and pen for each member of the group

Supply each group member with a postcard and a pen. Ask the group to put their name at the top of the postcard and then pass the card to the person on their right. Once this has been done, ask the person holding the card to write down one thing that they appreciate about the person whose name appears at the top of the postcard. Then pass the card on to the person on the right and repeat the process until the person whose name is at the top of the postcard receives their own card.

Ask the card owners to read the comments that have been written about them.

- What did they think about the comments?
- Is it difficult to accept positive comments?

Ask the group if they found it difficult to write what they appreciate about another person.

- Why is it difficult?
- Would it be more difficult or easier to speak to the person directly?

3

Equipment: postcards
paper plates
shaving foam
large plastic sheet
blindfolds

Pick about ten cards and randomly write either: north, south, east or west on each card. On another set of cards write a number from 1 to 10. Prepare a number of paper plates by spraying a large mound of shaving foam onto the plates. Spread the large plastic sheet over the floor. Ask for several volunteers from the group. Blindfold each of the volunteers and ask them to remove their shoes and socks. Place the paper plates in a random pattern onto the floor covering.

Position each volunteer at various points around the room. Select another member of the group and ask them to choose a direction card (N S E W) and ask another group member to select a number card. The first volunteer must face the direction indicated by the first card and then walk the number of steps as directed on the second card. Continue this for each volunteer.

You might like to have a bowl of water and a towel available!

4

Equipment: postcards
paper and pens

On the postcards write the following categories:

Short	Tall
Rabbit	Chicken
Stream	Pond
Athlete	Singer
Coffee	Tea
Porsche	Land-Rover

Divide the group in two and ask them to choose which of the categories they would like to be. For instance, if the categories chosen are 'Rabbit' and 'Chicken' then one half of the group will be rabbits and the other half chickens. You may need to 'help' the groups decide who is to be either the rabbit or the chicken. Give each group a sheet of paper and a pen and ask them to write down a list of qualities for their word. What are the benefits of being a rabbit? What's good about being a chicken?

Ask one member of each group to read their group's list of qualities and the other group can offer reasons why it is better to be in the other category.

Repeat the process with the other categories.

Ambition

1

Equipment: pen and paper for each group member

Tell the group it's now time for them to use a little bit of their imagination. (If they haven't got any, tell them to go home immediately and get it from under the bed or to try the delicatessen counter at the local supermarket!)

Ask the group to write on the piece of paper one thing that they would like to achieve in the next twenty years. (Any comments about still breathing or avoiding becoming a fossil should be ignored, or better still, display an 'Old is Beautiful' banner!)

Ask the group if they can think of anyone who has had a major achievement during the last couple of years. They might refer to a sports personality or musician, or someone they know who has achieved a long term ambition.

2

Equipment: paper and pens

Give each member of the group a piece of paper and a pen, and ask them to write three statements about their hopes or desires on the piece of paper (don't write any name or initials which might identify the writer). For example:

1. I want to build a boat.
2. I want to become an actor/actress.
3. I want to travel around the world.

When each group member has finished, collect the statements, shuffle them and then distribute them around the group. Ask one group member to read the three statements and see if the rest of the group can guess who wrote the statements. To add a little bit of mystery, have some statements already prepared which are not specific to anyone in the group. These statements could be based on someone you or the group know, or be entirely fictitious. Some of the statements could be totally bizarre!

3

Equipment: paper, pens and envelopes
flipchart

Distribute the paper and pens to the group. Have prepared a list (on the flipchart) of ten dreams or ambitions that you would like to achieve during the next ten years. Show the group your list of ambitions and chat about what you might do to achieve them.

Ask each member of the group to make a list, on their pieces of paper, of ten dreams or ambitions that *they* would like to achieve over the next ten years, for example career, qualifications, hobby, or relationships. If some of the group feel able, ask them to share with the others one or two of their ambitions and how they would go about achieving them.

Anger

1

Equipment: pen and paper for each group member
large sheet of paper and marker

Ask the group to think about all the things that make them angry – really angry. For instance, someone leaving their dirty socks on the table, or borrowing your toothbrush without asking.

Suggest to the group that they choose one of the things which makes them angry and write it on their piece of paper. Chat about the 'angry-making things', write some of them on the large sheet of paper and display it where everyone can see it. The group should keep their sheet of paper for later.

2

Equipment: small piece of paper and a pen for each member of the group
large sheet of red paper and pins or sticky tape

Introduce the theme by telling the group about the things which really irritate you. For instance, the top left off the toothpaste tube, an empty biscuit tin, somebody crunching a sweet in the cinema, dogs barking late at night or programming the video to tape your favourite film and then finding it has taped a documentary about slugs.

Ask the group about the things which irritate them. Get them to write these things down on their pieces of paper. Consider questions such as:

- Do these things always irritate me?
- Do I get more irritable when I'm tired?

- Do certain people make me irritable?
- Do I get irritable with other people when things haven't gone my way?

Now ask the group to pin or stick their pieces of paper to the large sheet of red paper.

Authority

1

Equipment: plastic beaker
pen
egg
cloth large enough to cover beaker

Announce to the group that you are going to perform a magic trick! Place the egg under the beaker and then cover the beaker with the piece of cloth. Tell the group that you are now going to use your magic to turn the egg into a chicken! Take the pen and wave it over the beaker. Say, in a theatrical voice, 'Eye of toad, nose of rhino with dark blue eyes, turn this egg into a chicken surprise!' Tap the beaker three times and then remove the cloth. Lift the beaker to reveal the egg. 'What, no chicken?'

Apologise to the group and tell them that your powers of magic seem to have left you. Ask the group if they have any idea why the egg didn't turn into a chicken. Once they have offered several ideas for your lack of success, explain to the group that you obviously have no authority over creation and nature. Perhaps we need to investigate someone who does!

2

Equipment: pack of playing cards

Deal one card, face down, to each member of the group. Ask them to look at their card. The person with the highest card (ace equals high) is asked to think of a task or errand which they would like to see carried out. The task or errand can be as wacky as they want it to be. Then the person with the lowest card is told that they have to carry out the task or errand at the end of the session. Alternatively, you could have some tasks already written on pieces of card. The tasks can be quite simple and carried out straight away, such as:

- do twenty press-ups with your nose
- sing a nursery rhyme backwards
- divide 1,000,000 by 14

The person with the lowest card simply takes, at random, one of the task cards. You can repeat this game as often as you want.

Ask the group what they thought about being asked to do wacky tasks. Did any of the group do them? If so, why? Have a brief discussion about the idea of authority. Who said the tasks had to be done? What would have happened if some-one had refused to do a task?

Baptism

1

Equipment: a large plastic bowl
4-6 jam jars each filled with coloured water
(use food colouring)

On each of the jars place a sticky label which has a snappy title such as 'licky lemon', 'gungy green', 'bluebottle blue', 'risky red'. Have the jars displayed as the group arrive. Don't mention anything about the jars until everyone has arrived and they are wondering what the jars contain. Announce to the group, with enthusiasm, that you have discovered a way of recycling mouthwash! The colours are, in fact, flavours which help disguise the previous flavour! Ask the group if anyone would like to try your recycled mouthwash. If anyone dares, the plastic bowl is there to empty the contents of their mouths into!

Explain to the group that the jars only contain coloured water but you are working on a way to recycle toothpaste and you will let them be the first to test!

Ask the group if they know what products use water? (Mouthwash! shampoo, fizzy drinks, soups.) What do we use water for? (Washing, cleaning the car, drinking, making tea and coffee.)

2

Equipment: large plastic bowl filled with warm water
bar of soap
plastic bag filled with wet mud (or you could use cocoa powder mixed to a paste)

Display the bowl of water on a table at the front of the room. Put your hands into the bag containing mud/cocoa and enthusiastically cover your hands in the mixture. Tell the group that someone told you that covering your hands with this mixture would improve the look of the skin. Once you have covered your hands (keeping the mixture on your hands) go to one of the group and ask them to shake your hand and tell you if your hand feels softer! Ask why they won't touch your hand.

Ask the group if any of them would like the mixture put on their face. Now wash the mixture off! Will anyone shake your hand now?

Ask the group what the problem was with having 'dirty' hands. Why did they feel uncomfortable about touching the mixture? Why did washing your hands make a difference?

Christian life _____

1

Equipment: one glass jar
small amount of flour
sticky label
pen and paper for each member of the group

Once all the group have arrived, pick up the glass jar and begin to examine it very carefully. Unscrew the lid and shake the jar so that some flour is thrown into the air. Look at the underside of the lid and read the sticky label: 'Danger! Highly infectious bacteria. Do not breathe dust. Contamination is fatal!' Look at the group and offer a mumbled apology: 'Sorry, looks like we're all going to die in a few minutes. This may be the last chance we have to write a message to someone.'

Distribute pens and paper. Ask the group to think about what they would write as their very last message. For example:

- Would it be a letter to say sorry?
- Would it be a letter to someone they loved?
- Would it be a letter to put something right with someone?
- Would it be a letter to tell someone exactly how they felt about an issue?
- Would it be a letter to an influential person, politician or world figure?

2

Equipment: postcard for each member of the group

On each postcard write *one* letter from the alphabet. Either allow each group member to take a card at random (have the cards face down), or tape a card under each seat. If the group is fairly small, simply ask them to get their cards and try and make as many words as they can using some or all of the cards. If the group is large enough, give each member of the group a number. Call out a sequence of random numbers and those members must try and form a word from their letters.

When you have finished ask the group what was difficult about the game.

3

Equipment: small jigsaw puzzle for each group (you could make these by cutting up old birthday or Christmas cards)

Divide the large group into several smaller groups, each containing about three to four people. Give each group one of the jigsaws and ask them to put the jigsaw together with the picture face down. They are not allowed to look at the cover of the jigsaw box or look at the picture on the jigsaw pieces. Try not to have jigsaws with too many pieces – it could take for ever!

Once the groups have finished, ask them what it felt like to have nothing to refer to when trying to complete the jigsaw. If you have time, get the groups to swop jigsaws and put them together using the picture.

- Did the group find this easier?
- Why was that?

4

Equipment: large sheet of paper and a marker pen

When the group have arrived, appear to be in an extreme state of excitement. Announce to the whole group that you didn't give any money to the Church last week. Instead you spent the money on some lottery tickets and . . . guess what . . . you didn't win!

Explain that you nearly won. In fact, you would have won if you'd guessed the right numbers!

Write the figure £1,000,000 on the large sheet of paper. Ask the group to list some of the things that they would buy if they won that amount of money. Once you've got quite a long list, look it over and circle all those items that are for personal use only, such as: car, house, jewellery.

- Were there any listed items left which would be bought for other people?
- Why do we think about what we want to buy for ourselves first?
- Is it easy to think about giving some of the money away? Why?

5

Equipment: bag of doughnuts
rubber bands

Tie the rubber bands together so that you have a rubber 'rope' about a metre long. Attach the 'rope' to the doughnut. Ask the group to form pairs. While one of the pair is lying on their back, the second person stands on a chair and attempts to 'feed' the doughnut to their partner by bouncing the doughnut towards their partner's mouth. The person lying on the floor is not allowed to move or lift their head at any time. If you're feeling 'kind' the person feeding their partner can bounce the doughnut with their hand. If you want to add a good dose of fun, get the 'feeder' to hold the rubber 'rope' between their teeth and then attempt to feed their partner. It's not compulsory, but you might like to have something to help the person being fed to clean themselves afterwards.

6

Equipment: paper and pens

Ask the group to stand in a circle (if you have a large group, two circles). Ask each group member to hold their hands out, at waist level, and, with their right hand, grasp the hand of the person on their left and with their left hand, grasp the hand of the person on their right. If they've done this correctly, everyone in the circle should be joined together. The object of the game is to try and uncross everyone's hands without letting go of their partners' hands. At the finish, everyone should still form a circle and remain joined together, but with their hands at their sides.

This can be a difficult game and may not be easy for any group members who have a problem with mobility.

7

Equipment: clip-on clothes pegs

Divide the group into three categories: Grabbers, Givers and Goodies. Distribute the clip-on clothes pegs so that every group member has the same number of pegs and ask everyone to put the pegs anywhere on their clothes as long as they are visible (the more pegs each member has the better).

At a given signal, the three groups go around and behave as their name implies. The 'Grabbers' try and take as many pegs as they can and put them onto their clothing, the 'Givers' simply offer their pegs to anyone and the 'Goodies' try and take the pegs that the 'Grabbers' have taken and give them back to the original owner!

It might be advisable to suggest that you are not liable for any torn clothing!

8

Equipment: none required

Ask the group to sit in a circle with two chairs back to back in the centre of the circle. Ask for two volunteers: one to be a counsellor, the other to be a telephone caller with a problem. Choose one of the scenarios below and ask the two volunteers to act out their roles. The telephone caller explains their problem and the counsellor offers some advice. The caller can add to or question any of the advice that the counsellor offers.

At an appropriate moment, end the role-play and ask the rest of the group what they thought of the advice.

Scenario 1
It's next door's dog. It barks all day and whines all night. The people next door go out to work and leave the dog on its own. When they arrive home after work, they let the dog out into the garden and it goes mental. It runs around, barking, jumping up at the fence and growls if any of us go into our garden.

Scenario 2
It's exam time again. I've tried my best to revise but it's been really difficult to find enough time to study all the subjects. I've tried talking to some of my friends but they seem too busy to spend any time chatting. I've even taken some of my revision books with me to my part-time job at the local store. The trouble is, it's very busy most of the time and I rarely get the chance to take a break and look at my books.

Scenario 3
It's this boy/girl at school/college. I think they're the best thing I've seen since banana and custard. I'd like to let them know

how I feel but I'm too embarrassed. What if they don't feel the same way? Yesterday someone told me that this boy/girl has got a dodgy reputation. They expect you to go all the way on the first date.

The group discussion should try to look at the situation from both sides. What would the group do if they found themselves in a similar situation?

9

Equipment: cards

Once the group have arrived, give each of them a number (say, 1-10) and two cards, each with a different letter of the alphabet written on them. Call out three numbers, and ask the group members who were given those numbers to get together. Call out another three numbers and so on until the group are in teams of three. The object of the exercise is for each team to use their letters to make as many words as possible in the time given. Allocate a scoring system which rewards longer words, e.g. two letters = 1 point, three letters = 2 points, four letters = 3 points and so on. The team with the highest score are declared the winners.

Being presented with random letters and a task to complete is always a challenge. What were some of the problems the teams encountered?

10

Equipment: postcards
pen and paper for each group member
large sheet of paper in the shape of a question mark

Give each group member a piece of paper and a pen. Read one of the 'problems' from the postcards (have the 'problems' (below) written prior to the session). Ask the group to write on their piece of paper what their response would be. After you have posed all the 'problems' ask the group to discuss the issues as a whole, and attempt to arrive at a group response for each 'problem'.

Problems:

1. You have just discovered that your best friend is cheating on their partner. Help! What do you do?

2. You are browsing in a charity shop and find a twenty-pound note on the floor. Help! What do you do?

3. A friend has given you a computer disk containing a copy of an assignment, which you haven't done any work for. The assignment is due in tomorrow. Help! What do you do?

4. It's late, there's not a lot of people or traffic around. One of your mates offers to let you have a drive of their car even though you're too young to drive. Help! What do you do?

5. The restaurant is busy and the waiter has miscalculated your bill. You are being asked to pay ten pounds less than you should be charged. Help! What do you do?

6. Your dad has loaned you his mobile phone because you have run out of credit on your phone. He tells you to use it only in an emergency. You've got loads of friends who you need to call or text. Help! What do you do?

7. Your brother let you borrow his portable mini-disc player. You left it on the table while you had a drink of orange and, somehow, spilt juice all over his mini-disc player. You've wiped off as much of the juice as you can but the disc player doesn't seem to work properly. Help! What do you do?

8. A wrinkled relative has given you a hand-knitted, multi-coloured scarf for your birthday. Even your mum can't suppress a giggle. The relative is expecting you to wear the scarf the next time you visit. Help! What do you do?

9. A friend has drawn some pictures of a teacher, which are very funny but are likely to humiliate the teacher. The pictures have begun to appear all over school. Help! What do you do?

10. You've managed to put some blue dye into the shower-head in the bathroom. The joke is intended for your brother but your mum has gone into the bathroom to have a shower first. Help! What do you do?

The group discussion should not attempt to find the 'right' solution to the problem, but agree as a group about what they really would do in that situation.

Ask the group to fold their pieces of paper and pin them to the paper 'question mark', which can then be placed on the wall.

Confidence

1

Equipment: postcards and pen

On each of a series of postcards write one of the following:

Snails	Teddy bears	
Making paper planes	Ice-cream	
Jelly babies	Apples	
Flowers	Toffees	
Solar power	Parachuting	
Plastic spoons	Light bulbs	
Lawn mowers	Dogs	Worms

Give each member of the group a number, up to the number of postcards used. Choose a number and give the corresponding group member one of the cards. The group member has ten seconds to look at the card and must then speak for thirty seconds about the topic on the card. They are not allowed to use any delaying tactics or pause during their thirty seconds. If someone pauses or runs out of words then that person is out of the game. Continue playing until all the cards are used up or there is a clear winner.

Consider the following:

- Was it easy?
- How difficult did the group find talking about an unusual topic?
- What were the problems?

2

Equipment: selection of squeaky toys
blindfolds

Mark out an area as large as your room/space allows. Place the squeaky toys randomly around the selected area. Ask three or four volunteers from the group to leave the room. While the volunteers are out of the room, ask another member of the group to 'rearrange' the toys (just in case one of the volunteers thinks they may have been clever and tried to memorise the position of the toys). Blindfold the first volunteer and bring them back into the room. Explain to the volunteer that their task is to walk from one end of the marked area to the other without stepping on any of the toys.

At this point insist that the rest of the group be quiet and not attempt to try and 'advise' the volunteer.

Once the volunteer has completed the task, count the number of 'squeaks', if any, that they made during their attempt. Invite the next blindfolded volunteer into the room and repeat the task. The person who completes the task with the fewest 'squeaks' is awarded a squeaky toy as a reminder of their 'squeakless' ability.

3

Equipment: postcards
stopwatch

Make sure that you have enough postcards for each member of the group. Before you get together write one of each of the following on the postcards:

Wild boar	Wart hog	Camel	Lamb	Slug
Orang-utan	Sloth	Hen	Earthworm	
Moth	Seagull	Pheasant	Crocodile	
Anteater	Termite	Tortoise	Cat	

Give each member of the group a postcard with one of the animal names written on it. The idea of the game is for one group member to start a story containing a reference to the animal named on their card. The group member has twenty seconds to tell the beginning of the story and then the person next to the first group member must carry on the story, remember to refer to the first animal mentioned and also include the animal named on their card. The next person must then refer to the previous two animals and include their named animal in the story. The story continues with each new person referring to the animals previously mentioned and including their own animal. Remember that each story-teller has only twenty seconds to tell their part of the story including references to all the other previously mentioned animals. The last group member must finish the story to include every named animal. The time allowed for each storyteller is important. The first few group members should have little difficulty mentioning the previous animals but the last few storytellers will find it increasingly hard to remember and include every animal.

4

Equipment: flipchart
                pen

This activity should possibly come with a health warning! Write the word 'CHURCH' on the flipchart. Ask the group how they could make church unattractive, boring, a turn-off, irrelevant and uninviting. In other words, how could they stop people coming to church (or not want to attend in the first place!).

Write the group's responses on the left-hand side of the page. Now, take each of the responses and, on the right-hand side of the page, write the opposite to the original response. For instance, if someone suggested 'preach for hours', then the opposite would be: 'short, sharp talks'.

See how you go, but don't feel offended if some of the group's initial responses are all too familiar to your church!

Death

1

Equipment: paper and pens

Give each group member a piece of paper and a pen. Ask them to think about what they would write on their own headstone. For example: 'I kept telling them I was ill' or 'Back in five minutes' or even 'I'll be lucky to get out of this alive'. Suggest to your group that they might like to think of epitaphs that say something either about what they would like to have achieved or about their personality.

Have a chat about how group members would like to be remembered. Are there any specific things they would like to do, or see done, before they die?

2

Equipment: piece of string
sticky tape
paper
pens

As each member of the group arrives, give them a piece of paper and a pen. Ask them to write their name on the paper. As they do this place the piece of string along the length of the room and stick each end down with the tape. Mark one end of the string: 'Dead, buried and that's it' and the other end of the string: 'Journey's end'. Ask the group to consider the question: 'Is death the end of our existence or is there something more?'

After a few moments ask the group to stand somewhere along the string which corresponds with their idea or thoughts of 'life after death'. If any of the group are unsure, which you should stress isn't a problem, then they are to stand somewhere in the middle of the string. If any of the group think there may be an afterlife but aren't certain, then they should stand nearer to 'Journey's end'. And if any of the group think an afterlife is possibly stretching things a bit too far, then they should stand nearer to the 'Dead and buried' end. Once they are all satisfied with their position, then ask them to stick, using the tape, their name onto the string indicating where they stood.

Decisions

1

Equipment: 10-12 postcards

Take two of the postcards and on one write 'NO' and on the other write 'YES'. On the remaining postcards write the following questions, or create your own.

1. Should I paint my toe nails bright green?
2. Should I give all my money to charity?
3. Should I shave my head?
4. Should I wear purple lipstick?
5. Should I have my belly button pierced?
6. Should I wash my face with baked beans?
7. Should I wear a pair of blue fluffy slippers?
8. Should I wear a dress next week?

Take the question cards and place them face down in front of you. Shuffle them around and then invite one of the group to choose a card. Take the two other cards with 'No' and 'Yes' written on them. Place them both face down in front of the volunteer. Ask the volunteer to close their eyes while you shuffle the two cards around. When you are ready, ask the volunteer to pick one of the cards using the 'eeny, meeny, miny, mo' method. Ask the volunteer to turn over the card they have chosen to see what their answer will be!

Repeat the process until all your question cards are used up. The results should be good for a laugh!

2

Equipment: sheet of paper and pen for each group member

Ask the group to write their responses to the following situations. Encourage them to be as honest as they can as no one will be reading their completed sheets. Read each of the situations below, allowing approximately one minute for each group member to write their response.

1. You open your Christmas present to find it is an awful pair of socks with pictures of cuddly bunnies on them.

2. A letter arrives telling you that you have just won a year's supply of chocolate.

3. You receive a telephone call telling you that you were unsuccessful in your application for the part-time job you applied for at the local music store.

4. On your way to the group meeting you slipped over and your jeans are covered in mud.

5. A well-known magazine publisher has written to you saying how impressed they were with the article you wrote for a major youth magazine. The publisher wants to know if you would consider writing a regular feature article on youth issues.

6. All your favourite clothes are still waiting to be washed and you have had to come to the group wearing a large plastic coat to hide your old clothes.

When the group have finished writing their responses, ask each member to fold their piece of paper and put it in their pocket or under the chair.

3

Equipment: bag of marshmallows

Prepare a series of questions and write them on the cards. Ask the group to divide into pairs. Nominate one of the pair to ask questions and the other to answer.

Sample questions (only require a 'yes' or 'no' answer):

1. Most lipstick contains fish scales. (yes)
2. Bats always turn left when leaving a cave. (yes)
3. Taphephobia is the fear of taps. (no, fear of being buried alive)
4. Pinocchio is the Italian for 'pine eye'. (yes)
5. The longest recorded flight of a chicken is two minutes. (no, 13 seconds)
6. Slugs have four noses. (yes)
7. A jellyfish is made out of silicon. (no, 95 per cent water)
8. In Tokyo, they sell toupees for dogs. (yes)
9. Fingernails grow nearly ten times faster than toenails. (no, four times faster)
10. Dolphins sleep with both eyes open. (no, just one eye open)

The person answering the question nods their head for a yes answer and shakes their head for a no. If they answer correctly they are given a marshmallow, BUT . . . they cannot eat it. The questioner places the marshmallow on their partner's tongue. The partner must keep their tongue sticking out until they have answered another question correctly, then they can eat the marshmallow. If they answer a question incorrectly, they have another marshmallow placed on top of the first. The questioner must not help their partner in any way! You might like to have the partners reverse roles after a few questions.

4

Equipment: selection of toilet rolls
squares of newspaper
blindfolds

Ask for three or four volunteers from the group. Explain to the volunteers that they are about to take part in a consumer test which may have an amazing impact on the development of future products.

Blindfold the volunteers and sit them to one side of the room. Lay out a selection of toilet rolls on a table. The selection should contain samples from as many different brands as possible. Try to have a range of samples which varies from total luxury to sheets of cut-up newspaper.

Ask one blindfolded volunteer at a time to feel the paper and then try and identify which is the luxury paper and which is the newspaper. Repeat with the other volunteers.

When you have completed the 'test' ask the volunteers to take off their blindfolds and now repeat the test. Was it easier to identify the different papers without the blindfold? Or was it just the same with and without the blindfold?

5

Equipment: sheets of paper and pens

Ask the group to write their responses to the following situations. Encourage them to be as honest as they can; no one will be reading their completed sheets. Read out each of the situations below, allowing approximately one minute for the group members to write their response.

1. Recently you told one of your best mates whom you fancied. A couple of days later, not only did half the town know your secret but, worst of all, the object of your desire had also been told.

2. Congratulations, it's your birthday! Aged Aunt Dotty has just given you a present. Your dad whispers that Aunt Dotty hasn't got much money and she had to save up for several weeks to be able to buy your present. When you open it, you discover a pair of furry slippers in a disgusting shade of pink.

3. A letter arrived in this morning's post telling you that you had an interview for a job.

4. Someone told you that today was bad-taste-clothes day and that all the group members would turn up wearing jumble-sale rejects. When you arrive, dressed in your wardrobe's worst, you realise that you've been the butt of a practical joke.

5. You are just looking through one of those top-shelf magazines, purely out of curiosity (!), when someone taps your shoulder. When you turn around your eyes meet those of the vicar.

6. Your family tell you not to worry too much about getting high grades in your exams. When the results come through you have achieved far better grades than anyone thought.

When the group have finished writing their responses, ask each member to fold their piece of paper and put it in their pocket.

6

Equipment: paper
                 pens

As each member of the group arrives, give them a piece of paper and a pen. Ask each of them to think of all their favourite foods, colours, music and pet/animal. They must not write their name on any part of the paper. Collect all the pieces of paper, shuffle them and then redistribute the paper to the group. In turn, ask one person to read the list on the piece of paper that they have. Nominate one person to try and guess who wrote the lists. Can they guess the author? If not, ask a second person and so on. Allow time for each piece of paper to be read and for one person from the group to try and guess who it is.

You could make it a little competitive by awarding points for each correct guess. Alternatively, have one person read one item from the list and see if anyone can guess the author. Use a scoring system that awards 10 points for a correct guess after one item, 8 after two, 6 after three and so on.

How easy or difficult was it to guess who wrote the lists? How well does each member of the group know the other members?

Doubt

1

Equipment: sheet of paper and a pen for each member

Ask each group member to write three statements about themselves on the piece of paper. Suggest that they make one statement true, one statement totally over the top and one statement believable, but not absolutely true (not necessarily in that order).

Ask each member of the group to read their 'statements'. Can the rest of the group decide which is true, which over the top and which is almost true?

If the group guess the 'almost true' statement, what made them doubt the truth of the statement? Was it a lucky guess or did something make them question the statement?

2

Equipment: child's short story book
bag of sweets
small squares of paper and card

As each member of the group arrives, give them a square of paper which has a number written on it. (Don't make it easy. Have numbers such as 1927, 6749 or 5463.) Don't tell anyone what the numbers mean. Begin to read the story. Try and use a boring voice which drones on and on. At intervals, drop one of the numbers into a sentence, for example 'And when Jack fell down the 6749'. If the person with the number responds, give them a sweet. Every second or third number, refuse to give the person a sweet even if they respond on hearing their number. Make the numbers and giving out sweets as random as possible so that none of the group are sure whether a response will earn them a sweet or not.

3

Equipment: paper
           pens

Give each member of the group a piece of paper and a pen. Ask them to write the word 'When' in capital letters at the top of the page. Each person is to write a 'when' descriptor. For example: 'It was Christmas time and . . .' or 'Just as the alarm clock sounded . . .' or even 'It was a dark and stormy night . . .'. When they have completed this ask them to fold the piece of paper so that the 'when' descriptor is concealed and pass the paper on to the person immediately on their left. This person writes 'Where' on the paper in capital letters and suggests an idea for a place. For instance 'On the carpet . . .' or 'In the middle of the shopping centre' or even 'In the back of a pick-up truck . . .'. The same process is used as before with the paper folded to conceal the 'where' suggestion and the paper is passed on for a third time. The next person then writes the word 'Why' in capital letters and proceeds to write an explanation as to 'why'. Again, for example, 'Because she didn't like doughnuts' or 'Because the boy next door had a large bag of carrots for sale' or even 'Because the next-door neighbour's cat had just given birth to kittens'.

Pass the completed paper to the next person and then read the results!

4

Equipment: flipchart
           paper and pens for each group member

Display the following quiz on the flipchart:

1. gnikool
2. your hat
   keep it

3. keen surgeon

4. take
take

5. ban   ana

6. options, options, options, options, options.

7. man
___
board

8. r/e/a/d/i/n/g/

9. X X

10. 21 October/21 October

Distribute the paper and pens and ask each member of the group to try and work out what each of the ten puzzles means.

The answers are:

1. Looking backwards	6. Several options
2. Keep it under your hat	7. Man overboard
3. Sharp operator	8. Reading between the lines
4. Double take	9. Double cross
5. Banana split	10. Double date

You might like to give the group this example before they attempt the puzzle:

GROUND
Feet
Feet
Feet
Feet
Feet
Feet

Answer = six feet underground!

Faith

1

Equipment: postcards

Write one of the statements below on each postcard.

1. A giraffe can clean its ears with its 52-centimetre tongue.
2. Fingernails grow nearly four times faster than toenails.
3. Clinophobia is the fear of beds.
4. A mole can dig a 100-metre tunnel in just one night.
5. Slugs have four noses.
6. A sneeze travels out of your nose at over 100 miles per hour.
7. The elephant is the only mammal that can't jump.
8. More *Monopoly* money is printed in a year than real money.
9. More people use blue toothbrushes than red ones.
10. No piece of paper can be folded in half more than seven times.

Give the cards to group members and ask them to read the statement on the card. They can then ask the rest of the group whether they think the statement is true or false. (All the statements are true . . . check them out!)

2

Equipment: card

You will need an even number of pieces of card. On one piece of card draw a series of interlocking shapes, similar to a puzzle. Copy the 'puzzle' onto a second card. Taking another card, draw a different 'puzzle' and again copy the 'puzzle' onto another piece of card. Repeat the process until you have used all the cards. On the 'original' set of cards, cut out the interlocking shapes leaving a completed copy for each 'puzzle'.

Divide the group into pairs. Have the pairs sit back to back so that they cannot see each other's 'puzzle'. One of the partners has the copy of the 'puzzle' while the other has the cut out pieces. The partner with the copy 'puzzle' tries to describe each piece of the 'puzzle' and where to place it.

What difficulties did the group have completing the 'puzzles'?

Fear _____

1

Equipment: sliced loaf
butter and jam
knife and small plate

Have the loaf, butter and jam on display as the group arrive. Announce to the group that you have recently discovered the delights of eating bread and jam; you can't think of anything better to eat for breakfast, lunch, tea and supper. In fact, so obsessed are you with bread and jam that you have given up all other forms of food. But you have decided that this obsession is possibly a bit too silly. After all, jam every day? You need the group to help you out. Can they suggest some different toppings for the bread?

Make a list of their suggestions. Now tell the group that a thought has just struck you. Given the additives that are put into some bread and the different types of bread (white, wholemeal, granary and so on), you think it might be safer to buy the wheat grain before the farmer has sown it! Can you still serve the grain with the toppings the group suggested?

The group should tell you that the wheat grain has to be planted, has to germinate, grow and be harvested, ground into flour and then baked. Ask them why all this has to take place.

2

Equipment: large sheet of paper and a marker pen

Ask the group to think about items that are fragile, such as glass, paper, ice, skin. Write all their ideas down one side of the large sheet of paper. Once you have a fairly long list, ask the group to list things that would break or damage the fragile items that have already been listed. Write these items against the fragile items. (You can use the same item against as many fragile items as you want.)

Some of the suggestions may include thermonuclear devices which deal with the whole list! Or include stones, metal, cars and so on.

Discuss with the group how some of the fragile items get broken or damaged.

• Is it accidental or intentional.

• Can we do anything to avoid accidental or intentional damage?

3

Equipment: flipchart

Write a list of phobias from the selection below. Don't write the meaning of the phobia, that's for the group to try and guess.

Monophobia	(fear of loneliness)
Nyctophobia	(fear of the night)
Zelophobia	(fear of jealousy)
Ergophobia	(fear of work)
Algophobia	(fear of pain)
Scopophobia	(fear of being looked at)
Ochlophobia	(fear of crowds)
Thanatophobia	(fear of death)
Kakorraphiaphobia	(fear of failure)
Odontophobia	(fear of teeth)

The group might have a lot of fun just trying to pronounce some of these words!

Reveal one phobia name at a time and see if the group can guess what the phobia is a fear of. You might like to have a go at inventing some of your own phobias, e.g. footaphobia (fear of football), brussophobia (fear of brussels sprouts) or even soapophobia (fear of soap operas).

Forgiveness

1

Equipment: postcards

Prepare three postcards for each member of the group. One postcard will have 'Forgive' written on it, the second will have 'Sometime, maybe' written on it and the final card will have 'Never' written on it.

Read the following scenarios to the group and, after each one, ask the group whether they would forgive. Each member of the group will then 'vote' to show how they would respond.

1. Jenny has just telephoned her boyfriend to tell him she's pregnant. He's furious and blames Jenny for not being 'careful'. She apologises but tells him she's sometimes so tired at night that two or three days can go by without her taking the pill. Her boyfriend slams the phone down. Jenny doesn't hear from him for six weeks. Suddenly, late one night, he telephones and says he's sorry and can she forgive him for reacting the way he did?

2. Tony has been saving for a two-month walking holiday in Scandinavia. He only needs to work at his part-time job for five more weeks and he'll have enough money saved. Just as he's about to leave work one Thursday evening Tony's boss calls him to one side and informs him that because work is slow at the moment he can't afford to employ Tony any longer. Tony's furious and demands that he be allowed to work for the next five weeks as he was promised. The boss refuses. Tony walks home wondering whether he should forgive his boss and go and apologise.

3. Ben is a soccer fanatic. He's just been invited, with his best friend Dan, to go for a trial with a local team. When they

arrive at the training ground Ben realises that he's forgotten his soccer boots. He remembers that his friend's boots are the same style and size as his own. While his best friend chats to the coach, Ben opens his friend's bag and takes the soccer boots. Ben plays in the training match while his friend watches from the bench. Ben gets selected to play for the team. His best friend receives a polite 'thanks, but no thanks'. Ben is really happy to get chosen for the team but his friend, although not upset at not getting selected, thinks Ben's behaviour was out of order. He isn't sure how to respond to Ben.

After the group have 'voted' in each scenario, ask them why they chose to vote the way they did.

2

Equipment: cards

Hand out the cards with the sentences below:

- The monkey escaped but . . .
- When Aunt Ethel saw the mess she . . .
- Dad went absolutely ballistic when he saw the car but . . .
- If I ever see him/her again I'll . . .
- The doctor said that it'd be OK in a few years' time so I said . . .
- When I woke up and saw what had happened I . . .
- It wasn't so much the money but the fact that she'd painted my feet pink. When I see her I'll . . .

You might like to think of other slightly wacky scenarios. The idea is for the group member to read the sentence and conclude the story which *must* include the word 'forgiveness' somewhere. It doesn't necessarily mean that the story concludes with someone being forgiven. Encourage the group to let their imaginations run riot.

Freedom

Equipment: none required

Divide the group into two teams. Team A must choose six film titles. Team B have to guess what the title is by asking yes-or-no questions. For example: 'Is it a romance?'; 'Does it involve a dog?'. Team B are given five attempts (questions) to guess the film title correctly. If they fail to guess the film, then one of the team must 'go to prison' and sit away from the group and not contribute to their team. If Team B correctly guess the film title then they can 'release' a team member already in prison or, if they haven't got a team member in prison, they can use the correct guess to 'get out of prison free'. You might like the teams to swap over after a few minutes.

Friendship

1

Equipment: sheets of paper
              pens

Give each member of the group a pen and piece of paper. Ask them to draw a line down the centre of the page. On the left-hand side of the paper they write down all those characteristics which they feel are good qualities in a friend, and on the right-hand side of the page all those characteristics which they don't consider to be positive qualities in a friend.

Once the group have completed this activity individually, ask them to form small groups of two or three members and compile a short list of the qualities that they feel a friend should have.

Now, as a whole group, try to define what 'friendship' really is.

2

Equipment: pen and paper for each member of the group
              flipchart

Give each member of the group a piece of paper and a pen. Ask them to think about all the things that they find difficult to tolerate in other people. For instance, cultural behaviour, accents or eating habits.

Suggest to the group that they choose one particular thing which they find most annoying and write it on their piece of paper. Chat about some of the 'annoyances' and write some of them onto the flipchart.

Gossip

Equipment: six postcards

Write one of the descriptions below on each postcard.

1. To increase spending, large retail companies spray all paper money with an invisible substance that reacts with human skin to produce an irritation. The result is that we have an overwhelming desire to get rid of the irritant (money) as quickly as possible.

2. If you stare at the sky long enough you can make it go dark.

3. The Government is thinking of introducing square wheels on all vehicles as an alternative to spending large amounts of money on traffic-calming road 'humps'. It is also hoped that the square wheel will reduce the number of deaths caused by speeding vehicles.

4. Staring at a clock will cause it to slow down.

5. A well-known furniture store is to introduce a tubular, floor-mounted filing system. People will be able to store all their documents simply by dropping them into the opening at the top of the tube. All the documents will then be sorted automatically by a small photo-sensitive device which files each document alphabetically.

6. A new computerised oven is about to appear in selected stores. The new ovens will be able to inform you of the number of calories your food contains and suggest an alternative recipe using non-fattening ingredients.

Give the cards to group members who can talk freely without getting tongue-tied. The idea is for one group member at a time to persuade the other group members that the statement written on their card is true.

Honesty

1
Equipment: none required

Arrange for one of the group to act as your assistant for this activity. You will need to have a quick rehearsal before you attempt this experiment in artificial stupidity!

Ask one of the group to think of a number between one and ten. That member of the group then whispers the number to your 'assistant'. Announce to the group that you will now tell them what the number is.

Ask your assistant to sit down on a chair. Place your hands on the assistant's head with your thumbs on their jaw, just below their ears. Ask your assistant to concentrate on the number they were given. While they are doing this, you must look around the room and stare for a few seconds at any object, then move on to stare at something else. As you are doing this, your assistant should clench his/her teeth together the number of times that corresponds to the number chosen. When you have finished counting, suddenly smack your hands together (preferably after removing them from your assistant's head) and tell the rest of the group the number.

Perform this as often as you wish or until someone guesses how you're doing it!

2
Equipment: paper and pens

Give each member of the group a piece of paper and a pen. Ask them to write down what they think the speaker really means in each instance. For example, 'I didn't see you there, honest' might mean 'I was hoping you wouldn't see me' or 'Wasn't it obvious I was trying to avoid you?'. 'It really doesn't hurt' might mean 'I've got thirty seconds to live' or 'It's less painful having teeth pulled out'.

Sentences:

1. It was a bargain.
2. You look wonderful.
3. This tastes gorgeous.
4. You wouldn't understand.
5. That's a great idea.
6. He/she wasn't my type.

When everyone has finished writing their definitions, read the first sentence and ask each member of the group to read out their definition. Repeat for each of the sentences.

3

Equipment: pens
paper

Distribute pens and paper to the group. Explain that it is often extremely difficult to understand what some people are trying to say or precisely what they mean. For instance, if someone were to say that they were 'Drouthy', would any-one know what they meant? (Drouthy means to be thirsty.) Ask the group to try and work out what the following words mean and write their *definitions* on the paper:

ASSOT	(Stupid)
MAW-WALLOP	(Badly cooked)
WOWF	(Really stupid)
FRAMPOLD	(Boisterous)
SORNER	(To scrounge)

CURKLING	(To cry)
GELID	(Cold)
GOTCH-GUT	(Fat)
PUKKA	(Genuine)
FUGLE	(To cheat)
FRANGIBLE	(Delicate)
NINNYHAMMER	(Fool)
BRINDIZE	(To drink)
BARRELASS	(To fall)
LOOBY	(Clumsy)

And yes, all of the words are real but not used too often!

Once you've finished reading all of the words ask the group to give some of their definitions before you reveal what the word really means!

4

Equipment: postcards
     paper
     pens

Write statement one (below) on the first postcard, statement two on the second postcard and so on until all the statements have been written on postcards (you might like to add some of your own statements too).

1. Over 2500 left-handed people are killed each year in the USA, from using products made for right-handed people.

2. If you were to count for 24 hours a day, it would take 31,688 years to reach one trillion.

3. A crocodile always grows new teeth to replace the old teeth.

4. The sentence: 'The quick brown fox jumps over the lazy dog,' uses every letter of the alphabet.

5. The only fifteen-letter word that can be spelt without repeating a letter is 'Uncopyrightable'.

6. A hedgehog's heart beats 300 times a minute on average.

7. Camels have three eyelids to protect themselves from sand blowing into their eyes.

8. Ancient Egyptians slept on pillows made of stone.

9. Around 1000 BC, most Egyptians were dead before their thirtieth birthday.

10. Every time you lick a stamp you are consuming one tenth of a calorie.

Give each member of the group a piece of paper and a pen. Distribute the cards, one to each member of the group, and ask them to read the statement on the card. They then ask the rest of the group whether they think the statement is true or false. After each statement each group member writes their answer on the piece of paper. Once all the statements have been read you can reveal that they are all true. Total the scores and see who has the most correct answers.

5

Equipment: pen and paper for each group member

Give each member of the group a pen and a piece of paper. Ask them to think about one possession that means more to them than anything else they own. Write the item onto the piece of paper, fold the paper in half and place the collected papers onto a table or other surface. Shuffle the papers and select one at random. Read the item to the group and they must decide whether to keep the item or get rid of it. Hopefully, the person who owns the item in question will try and persuade the rest of the group to keep it. Repeat the process with all the other items until you have reduced the number of 'kept' items. The object is to reduce the number of items until there is just one item left which the group have agreed to keep.

- What are the reasons for keeping this one remaining item?
- Is everyone agreed about this item?
- Was the process of getting rid of the other items difficult?

6

Equipment: paper and pen for each group member

Distribute the paper and pens to the group. Ask each member to write on the paper one fact about themselves that no one else in the group knows. For instance, 'When I was four, my brother pushed a piece of soap into my mouth because I called him a camel' or 'When I was six my mum made me have dancing lessons and I had to dress up as an apple at the Christmas show.' Tell the group not to write their name on the piece of paper.

After everyone has completed writing their 'fact', collect the papers and read one out at a time and see if the rest of the group can guess who it is.

Love

Equipment: large sheet of paper
broad-tip felt pen

Write the words 'LOVE IS . . .' on the sheet of paper. Ask the group to think about some definitions of love. For example: love is . . . kind. Write all the group's ideas on the paper. Don't ignore any of the ideas even though they may be a bit flippant.

Discuss some of the group's definitions. Can the definitions be put into categories, such as boy/girl relationships, brother/sister, parent/son/daughter, friend/friend, stranger/stranger? What does this tell us about our understanding of the word 'love'?

Love of God _____

1

Equipment: pen and paper for each member of the group

Ask the group to close their eyes for a few moments. While they have their eyes closed describe the following scene. Suggest to the group that it would be good if they can visualise the scene as you speak.

> It's a really cold miserable day. Dark grey clouds cover the sky and a fine mist is swirling around. As you look ahead there is a large bridge across a deep river. A man is standing on the bridge, staring at the sky. Suddenly the man climbs onto the bridge railings. He is having trouble keeping his balance but this doesn't seem to bother him. He seems in danger of falling off the bridge and into the river far below.
>
> Running over to him, not wanting to frighten him in case he falls, you ask him if he needs any help. Before you can say any more he shouts at you to keep away, threatening to jump if you come any closer.

Now ask the group to write on their pieces of paper what they would say to persuade the man to climb down from the bridge to safety. Discuss some of the responses.

2

Equipment: cards or paper, and pens

Explain to the group that you would like to start today's session with a reading from the Bible.

You will need to have prepared some paper or cards which contain the following Bible reading *but* with the underlined words omitted. The missing words are to be filled in by the group later in the session.

Love.

What if I could speak all languages of <u>humans</u> and of <u>angels</u>?

If I did not <u>love</u> others, I would be nothing more than a <u>noisy gong</u> or a <u>clanging cymbal</u>.

What if I could <u>prophesy</u> and understand all <u>secrets</u> and all <u>knowledge?</u> And what if I had <u>faith</u> that moved <u>mountains</u>?

I would be <u>nothing</u>, unless I <u>loved</u> others. What if I gave away <u>all</u> that I owned and let myself be <u>burnt alive</u>? I would gain <u>nothing</u>, unless I <u>loved</u> others.

Love is <u>patient</u>, never <u>jealous, boastful, proud</u> or rude.

Love isn't selfish or <u>quick-tempered</u>.

It doesn't keep a <u>record</u> of <u>wrongs</u> that others do. Love rejoices in the <u>truth</u>, but not in <u>evil</u>.

Love is always supportive, <u>loyal</u>, hopeful and <u>trusting</u>.

Love never <u>fails</u>!

1 Corinthians 13:1-8.

You might like to read the Bible verses again, slowly, emphasising the underlined words.

Perseverance

1

Equipment: Lego or similar building blocks
wastepaper basket

Divide the group into three or four teams. Give each team a box of building blocks and tell them that their task is to build a tower which will be strong enough to support a wastepaper basket (full or empty, it depends how tough you want to make the game). Before the game begins, choose one member from each team and ask them to behave as a saboteur in the building process. You might like to choose and brief the saboteurs before the session begins. The saboteurs are to make a nuisance of themselves by giving conflicting advice, knocking blocks over and causing as much hassle as they can. Advise the saboteurs that their behaviour should be planned carefully so as not to seem too obstructive, but enough to make it awkward for their team to complete the task.

After two minutes 'test' each construction with the wastepaper basket. It might help the saboteurs if you let the other team members in on the 'plot' to obstruct the building process.

Did any of the teams guess what the saboteurs were doing or did they genuinely think that the saboteurs were being a *real* 'pain'?

2

Equipment: fruit gums

Divide the group into pairs. Nominate one person from each pair to be the 'talker'. Arrange each pair so that they are directly opposite each other. The 'non-talker' is then asked to 'stick' their tongue out while you place a fruit gum on the tip of the tongue. The tongue must remain 'out' while the 'talker' begins to describe all their favourite foods. Encourage the 'talker' to describe each food in full detail giving as much emphasis as possible to taste and aroma. The object of the game is to see how long the 'non-talker' can keep their tongue extended with the fruit gum intact!

As soon as the 'non-talker' succumbs to the inevitable and eats the fruit gum, the pair change roles and the game begins again.

The winners are whoever can talk their partner into submission the quickest and whoever can resist their partner's 'sweet' talk the longest.

Problems

1

Equipment: sufficient paper and pens for each pair

Ask the group to divide into pairs and read them the following problem:

The disciples have walked for hours and have reached the banks of the River Jordan. Unfortunately they need to get to the other side without walking any further. There is no bridge in sight and the river is far too deep and wide to walk or swim across. Simon Peter looks across the river and sees two small boys playing on the other bank. Near the boys is a small rowing boat. The rowing boat can hold two boys or one disciple. After a while all the disciples succeed in crossing the river in the boat. How?

Answer: The disciples are on the east side of the river and the two boys are on the west. One of the boys rows the boat from the west side to the east side, gets out and one disciple rows back to the west side. The disciple gets out at the west side and the second boy rows back to the east side of the river. Both boys now row back to the west side. Repeat these four steps for every disciple carried from east to west.

2

Equipment: selection of envelopes and sheets of paper
           paper and pens

As the group arrive greet them with an abrupt 'hello' and carry on looking at the sheets of paper (which should be covered with numbers and lots of writing). Mutter something about 'parasites', 'piranha fish', 'financial carnivores' and such like. After a short while apologise to the group and tell them that you are having problems trying to sort out all the demands for your hard-earned money. Suggest that you feel totally besieged by the constant deluge of letters through your door. Have the group any ideas how you can 'sort out' your problems?

Return the few coins that the group collected for you (!) and give each of them a piece of paper and a pen. Ask the group to write down problems which they have experienced or are currently experiencing.

Ask the group how they feel when 'problems' occur which cause them to worry or become afraid of the future.

Self-image

1

Equipment: hand-out and pens, or overhead projector
paper and pens

Give each group member a copy of the following hand-out
(or use an overhead projector):

1. My friends think I'm . . .
   A. about as bright as a lump of coal
   B. quite clever
   C. a real genius
   D. out of this world
   E. could do with some ego deflating

2. I think I'm . . .
   A. a few slices short of a loaf
   B. a whole loaf short of a loaf
   C. a bakery
   D. loaf, butter and jam in one
   E. could do with some ego inflating

3. I can be persuaded by . . .
   A. flattery
   B. bribery
   C. raspberry jam
   D. common sense
   E. nothing if I don't want to be

4. I sometimes . . .
   A. act the fool to get attention
   B. get embarrassed in groups
   C. talk too much
   D. don't talk enough
   E. pretend to be something I'm not

5. If somebody doesn't agree with me I . . .
   A. make them look stupid
   B. pull a face
   C. agree to disagree
   D. try to convince them they are wrong
   E. listen to their opinion

Ask the group to tick the response which they feel is most like them or to add their own response. If you are using an overhead projector, they will need pen and paper to jot down their answers.

2

Equipment: two large sheets of paper (A3) or overhead projector and acetates

Draw the outline of a male on one sheet of paper or acetate and a female on the other. Discuss with the group what makes a good 'image', in other words, what do we need to look good to other people?

With an appropriate pen, draw on the person outlines the ideas of the group, for example hair-style, shoes, clothes, jewellery and accessories.

Ask the group what is important about the way we look.

• Does it matter how we look?
• Why should we follow any particular style or fashion?

3

Equipment: pens and paper for the whole group

Ask the group to 'pair up'. Give each person a pen and paper. Ask each pair to interview each other. What they *don't* need to find out are name, age, address or any other personal details. What they do need to find out are favourite foods, colours, music, hobbies, books, TV programmes and holiday destinations. Once this has been completed, collect the interview papers and redistribute them around the group. Ask each group member to read out the 'profile' they have been given. Can the rest of the group guess who the 'profile' belongs to?

4

Equipment: a piece of card for each member of the group

On each card write a job title. Use a variety of job titles, combining the sensible with the totally wacky! For example, doctor, teacher, politician, dustman, window cleaner, waiter, toilet attendant, couch potato, tea taster, deck chair attendant, pig farmer.

Give a card to each member of the group. Ask them to look at the card and, if they are happy with the job title, keep the card. If they would rather exchange it for another card, they can try and persuade someone else to exchange cards but neither person should know what is on the other's card!

When all the 'bartering' has finished ask the group how they felt about receiving the original card and, if they exchanged it, were they any happier with the new card?

5

Equipment: flipchart and marker pen

Announce to the group that you are going to a party during the week and you are a bit unsure what to wear. Can the group make any suggestions? Ask the group what they would wear if they were going to a really smart party. Make a list of the types of outfits and accessories. What kind of vehicle would each member of the group like to arrive in at the party? Would they invite the press and photographers to record the event of the year? Which magazines or news-papers would they like to see themselves in?

6

Equipment: paper and pens

Give each member of the group a piece of paper and a pen. Ask them to write at the top of the page: 'I wish I were/weren't . . .'

Chat about some of the things that you would like to change, either about yourself or about situations that annoy or worry you. Then ask the group to complete the sentence by writing two or three things that they would either change about themselves or situations they would like to alter in some way.

7

Equipment: postcards

Write each of the following phrases on a separate card:
1. I feel like a . . .
2. My mouth feels like a . . .
3. After eating, my stomach feels like a . . .
4. Every time I watch TV my head feels like a . . .
5. After I brush my teeth, they feel like a . . .
6. When I sneeze, my nose feels like a . . .

Now, on some of the other cards write:
1. hole in the road.
2. packet of cornflakes.

3. bottle of disinfectant.

4. bag of sawdust.

5. compost bin.

6. bucket of cold custard.

Shuffle the first set of cards and ask a member of the group to select one of the cards. To complete the sentence ask another group member to select a card from the second set of cards (make sure that these cards are face down). Now, read the complete sentence. Replace the used card from the second set of cards and shuffle. Repeat the selection process with other group members. The whole game should raise a laugh or three. You might like to write some of your own sentences and make the second set of cards as wacky as you can.

8

Equipment: bags of assorted children's clothes
cards, each of a different colour

Arrange the clothes into various bags. Make sure that most of the clothes are far too small for any member of the group. As the group arrive allocate each one a colour (red, blue, white, yellow, etc.). Depending on the number in your group, there should be some group members allocated the same colour.

Take the set of coloured cards, shuffle them, turn them so that the colours are face down and then ask one of the group to pick a card. Show the card to the group and every member who has been allocated that colour must, without looking, take an item of clothing from the bag and put it on.

Continue picking colour cards and getting the chosen group members to put on whatever item of clothing they pick out of the bag. After a while you should have every member of the group dressed in an assortment of ill-fitting clothes!

It might be fun to make the group continue to wear the clothing throughout the whole session!

9

Equipment: hand-outs and pens

Give each group member a copy of the following hand-out.

1. I think I'm . . .
   A. too easily influenced by other people
   B. pushy
   C. stubborn
   D. a chocolate addict
   E. a real fruit and nut

2. Sometimes I . . .
   A. say far too much
   B. don't say enough
   C. eat too many peanuts
   D. put my foot in it
   E. daren't say what I'm thinking

3. If I had the chance I'd . . .
   A. tell somebody exactly what I thought of them
   B. say sorry
   C. not do that again
   D. eat more raspberry jam
   E. try and be more positive

4. I . . .
   A. think I'm OK
   B. could do with a paper bag over my head

    C. want to learn to knit woolly socks
    D. shouldn't be so hard on myself
    E. need a bit of ego deflating

5. I think praying is . . .
    A. a waste of time
    B. talking to myself
    C. making me fall asleep
    D. a relationship with God
    E. for emergencies only

Ask the group to tick the response which they feel is most appropriate to them. They may feel like adding their own response. Encourage the group to be as honest as possible.

10

Equipment: pen and paper for each group member

This is a simple exercise, which might (not guaranteed) make you appear really cool to the group.

Give the group a pen and piece of paper each and ask them to think of a number and then write it onto the piece of paper. Insist that they show no one the number or tell anyone. Now, ask them to double the original number, multiply it by five, and then write the total at the bottom of the piece of paper.

Select any person in the group and ask them to tell you the total written at the bottom of their paper. Within moments you will be able to tell them their original number.

The trick is to take off the last digit of the number they give you. For example: if the original number is 26, doubling it gives 52, then multiplying by five gives you 260. Simply take away the zero and you have the original number. Neat, eh?

Serving God

Equipment: large cardboard box
four or five smaller boxes
tape, glue and paper-clips
straws, pipe-cleaners, bamboo canes and
thin wire
toy car or ball

Divide the group into four or five teams. Place the large box in the centre of the room. Arrange the smaller boxes in a circle with the large box in the centre. Each team is given a collection of tape, glue, paper-clips, straws, pipe-cleaners, canes and wire. The object is to build a bridge from the smaller box across to the large box in the centre (the distance between the large box and smaller ones depends on the space available and how difficult you want to make the task).

The winning team is the one whose bridge can support the toy car or the ball as it travels from the small box to the large box.

- How did the groups organise themselves?
- Were they successful?
- Why?
- What problems occurred?

Social justice

1

Equipment: paper and pen for each member of the group

Ask the group to think of a situation or issue which has been in the news recently and which has made them feel angry, annoyed or sad. Get them to write it down on a piece of paper. Is any member of the group willing to talk about what they have written?

- Why is it important to them?
- What do the rest of the group think?
- How would they go about changing the situation?

After you have listened to all the ideas, get the group to vote for the idea they consider to be the most important.

2

Equipment: postcards

Write one of the following words on each of the postcards:

Anger	Love	Jealousy	Happiness
Patience	Selfishness	Faithfulness	Kindness
Envy	Peacefulness	Troublemaker	

Give each member of the group a number, up to the number of postcards used. Choose a number and let the corresponding group member pick one of the cards at random. The group member has ten seconds to look at the card and then must speak for thirty seconds about the subject on the card. They are allowed to use a story, incident or something they've seen in a film or TV programme to try and describe what the word means. They are not allowed to use any delaying tactics or pause during their thirty seconds. If someone pauses or runs out of words then that person is out of the game. Continue playing until all the cards are used up or there is a clear winner.

3

Equipment: postcards

Distribute three postcards to each member of the group. You will have prepared the postcards before the session so that one card reads 'Agree', the second reads 'Disagree' and the third 'Don't know'.

Read each of the following statements and ask the group to respond by using one of the cards provided.

Statements:

1. It's OK to watch soft porn on TV; after all, didn't God create some very attractive bodies?

2. If someone is going to be offensive to other people then there's nothing wrong in being offensive to them.

3. Taking a day or more off work/school is just the same as stealing money from someone.

4. Cheating is OK if nobody finds out.

5. There's nothing wrong with driving at 50 miles an hour in a 30-mile speed limit.

6. It doesn't matter if you keep doing things that you know are dishonest or wrong because God will keep forgiving you.

After the group have voted for each statement, discuss each question and ask individual group members to defend their response.

Try to allow the group to reach a consensus of opinion. Offer your own perspective but don't let it dominate the thinking of the group as a whole.

4

Equipment: flipchart and pen

Write, in large letters, the word 'SIN' on the flipchart. Ask the group to discuss the idea of sin using some of the following questions:

- What is sin?
- Identify different actions or types of behaviour which are considered sinful.
- Are some forms of sin more or less acceptable than others?
- Is a type of behaviour considered acceptable by one person but sinful by another?
- Do we have to deal with sin?

Write some of the group's responses onto the flipchart.

5

Equipment: pen and paper for each group member

Give everyone a pen and piece of paper. Tell them that they have just been given £1,000 to spend. Ask them to write what would be on their spending spree list.

After they've done this, apologise and say that the money was not for them but to be spent on people who they consider to be in need of financial help (they are not to consider themselves in this!).

Once they've completed the second task, ask them how they felt when they were told that the money wasn't actually for them.

Time

Equipment: paper and pens
 flipchart

Give each member of the group a piece of paper and a pen. Write the following categories on the flipchart and ask the group to calculate how many minutes/hours each week they spend on each category.

Watching TV

Listening to music

Eating cereal

Having a shower

Eating chocolate

Picking fluff from between toes

Brushing teeth

Chewing gum

Staring out of window

Putting shoes on

Sleeping

Compare notes between the group. You might like to calculate the time for each category in a month/year/decade.

Trust

1

Equipment: small candle
box of matches
clear glass jam jar
large sheet of paper and marker pen

As you enter the room, or when all the group have arrived, walk over to the light switch and flick the switch on and off a few times, looking at the light bulb each time. After a short pause stroke your chin and mutter 'hmmm'. Say nothing more before you light the small candle with the matches and gaze at the flame. After a short time place the jam jar over the candle and wait for the flame to go out (which should happen very quickly). Look at the group and then at the candle and mutter 'hmmm' again. Ask the group why the candle went out. Someone should be able to tell you that the flame went out because of a lack of oxygen.

Pick up the jam jar (be careful as it may be hot), look into the jar and say, 'Where's the oxygen?' Hopefully, someone will explain that it's all around us, which is useful or else we would have a slight technical problem with breathing!

Ask the group how they know that the oxygen is all around us. What evidence do we have? For example, the ability to breathe!

Walk over to the light switch again and begin to switch it on and off. Ask the group how it works. (By electricity.) What evidence do we have that electricity exists? (Power to lights, heaters, TV, video, electric cookers and electricity bills!)

Now, ask the group what other things exist even though we can't see them. Make a list of the group's responses, such as smells, thoughts, sounds, the wind.

2

Equipment: postcards
blindfolds
chairs and objects

Write one of the following instructions on each postcard:

Turn left one step

Turn right one step

Go forward one step

Go backwards one step

Go forward two steps

Go backwards two steps

Have several copies of each instruction. Invite one member of the group to be blindfolded. Stand them in the centre of the room. Place a number of chairs or objects around the room. Shuffle the cards and ask another member of the group to take one card and read it aloud. The blindfolded member of the group must do exactly what the card tells them to do. Invite a second member of the group to read the next card and again the blindfolded member must do what the card tells them to do.

Repeat the process until all of the cards are used up or the blindfolded member cannot go any further. If the group member reaches a wall or chair, take another card until one gives them an opportunity to move away from the obstacle.

To make the game even more fun/difficult, have two or three people blindfolded and start them at different points of the room, each responding to the same card.

3

Equipment: flipchart or large sheet of paper and marker pen
sheet of paper and pen for every group member

Ask for a volunteer to draw on the flipchart. Ask for another volunteer who is to describe an object for the first volunteer to draw. The object should be something which has curves and straight lines, such as a car, train, telephone.

Ask the first volunteer to stand in front of the flipchart with their back to the rest of the group. The second volunteer should describe the object slowly and give instructions to the first volunteer who will attempt to recreate the object from the verbal directions. The second volunteer must not use any descriptive words which might give the first volunteer a clue as to the object's identity. Instructions must be 'draw a line twenty centimetres long', or 'draw a circle about the size of a dinner plate'. The fun will be seeing the completed object resulting from the instructions. Attempt this activity as many times as you want with different volunteers.

Ask the volunteers what it felt like to place their trust in what they were being told or placing their trust in someone else to carry out their instructions.

4

Equipment: postcards

Write one of the descriptions below on each postcard.

1. Bananas are, in fact, an alien life-form. Their leaders are so angry at so many of their people being eaten that they threaten to invade the earth tomorrow.

2. All plants can communicate with each other. To understand their language you need to be able to hear a certain audio frequency.

3. Computers have a personality and can get extremely upset when you get annoyed with them and may refuse to work.

4. If you stare at traffic lights long enough, you can make them change colour.

5. Some humans are evolved from a race of super moles. That is why some humans like to spend so much of their time crawling around in caves deep underground.

6. Dentists have been instructed by the Government to place a miniature micro-processor into one of our back teeth whenever we need to have a tooth filled. The micro-processor enables a Government department to locate us at any time.

Give the cards to group members who can talk freely without getting flustered. The idea is for one group member at a time to persuade the rest of their group that the statement written on their card is true.

5

Equipment: empty can of dog food, complete with label!
small cutlery fork
two Mars bars cut into small chunks
one small cup which will fit into the can of 'dog food'
flipchart

When the group has arrived and you are ready to begin, start to complain that you have been really busy today and haven't had time to eat since you woke up. On the way to the session you popped into a shop to buy something to eat. Unfortunately the only thing they had was a can of dog food. Well, the label said how nutritious the food was and that it kept dogs healthy, so what's good for a dog is good enough for you! Begin to eat from the can, using the fork. Chew away with a huge smile on your face, exclaiming how good the food tastes!

Ask if any of the group are hungry and would they like to try some of your food? Really encourage one or two of the group to try the 'food' and get them to agree that the food tastes good without them saying what they think the 'food' is. When you (or the group!) have had enough of the 'dog food', let everyone know that the 'food' was in fact a Mars bar.

Ask the group what thoughts went through their head as they watched you eat the 'dog food'. Why didn't some of the group accept your offer of sampling the 'food'? What made some of the group want to sample the 'food'? Why did they trust you? Write some of the responses down on the flipchart.

6

Equipment: pieces of card with instructions on

Prepare the cards so that each piece contains one of the following instructions:

Turn left	Turn right
Turn around	Stop
Move two paces	Move four paces
Balance on one leg	Close your eyes
Move forward	Move backwards
Say 'quack'	Put your fingers in your ears
Ignore the next command	Repeat the previous command
Move one pace to the left	Move one pace to the right

Shuffle the cards. Select at least four 'victims' and stand them at different locations in the room. Ask one of the group to choose three cards and 'victim' number one carries out the written instructions. Return the cards to the pack, shuffle and ask another member of the group to choose three cards for 'victim' number two. Repeat the process as often as you wish.

To make the game more 'active', prepare a set of cards for each 'victim' and have other members of the group read the instructions at the same time. This will result in all the 'victims' following the commands at the same time! Should be fun.

7

Equipment: cards

Write an instruction on each of the cards. Some ideas are listed below:

1. Stick your fingers in your ears and recite a nursery rhyme.
2. Touch your left foot with your right hand and your right foot with your left hand.
3. Stand on a chair and flap your arms up and down.
4. Try and touch your nose with your tongue.
5. Suck a sweet and hold your nose at the same time.
6. Walk around the room holding your ankles.
7. Sit on a chair and pretend to shiver. Wrap your arms around you and keep saying, 'It's so cold in here'.
8. Keep telling everyone that it's far too hot in the room. Ask to have the door and windows open.
9. Hold your head in your hands and tell everyone that there's going to be an explosion.
10. Form circles with your fingers, place them in front of your eyes, like binoculars, and ask everyone if they've seen the No. 45 bus.

Distribute the cards to the group and ask them to obey/ perform the instructions on the cards all at the same time.

Ask the group members how they felt about the instructions. Did any of the group refuse to take part? Why?

8

Equipment: glass bowl (shallow)
table-tennis ball
flour

Ask the group to divide themselves into pairs. Place the shallow glass bowl on the floor and put the table-tennis ball into the bowl. The first pair kneel opposite each other with the bowl between them. The object of the game is to see who can blow the ball out of the bowl first.

Continue with the other pairs and then have the winners from each pair compete against each other. Finally, have two unbeaten players ready to compete to find out who's the ultimate champion. However, just to make things a little more interesting, both players are to be blindfolded. Just before the players are ready to 'blow', tip a cup of flour into the bowl and let the game begin!

9

Equipment: pen and paper for each group member

Give each member of the group a pen and a piece of paper. Read out each of the following statements and ask them to write whether they think the statement is true or false.

1. St John was the only one of the 12 apostles to die a natural death.

2. A monkey was awarded a medal and promoted to the rank of corporal during World War 1.

3. Sliced bread was patented by a Mrs P. Ride in 1954.

4. An old custom, when drinking, was to throw a pinch of salt over your left shoulder to keep the devil away.

5. The cost of the first pay-toilets in England was one penny.

6. In 1647 the English Parliament abolished Christmas.

7. The word 'Abracadabra', used by stage magicians, was originally intended to cure hay fever.

8. In Victorian times there was a law which prohibited the wearing of a flat cap on a boat.

9. Gabriel and Michael are the only two angels to be named in the Bible.

10. The national flag of Austria was designed by an Irishman.

The answers are: 1. True; 2. True; 3. True; 4. False; 5. True; 6. True ;7. True; 8. False; 9. True; 10. False.

Total the scores and see who was able to make any sense (or good guesswork) of the strange statements.

10

Equipment: tubes of toothpaste
plastic cups
towels

Ask for three or four pairs of volunteers. Have one of the volunteers lay on the floor, face up, with the plastic cup held in their mouth. Spread the towel over their chest and shoulders. The partner stands over them and, without stooping or bending, attempts to empty the toothpaste into the cup.

A simple, fun game which might require some sort of prize to make the whole game worth while.

11

Equipment: photocopied sheets
pens

Copy the test paper below onto a master sheet and photocopy sufficient to have one sheet per person.

Give each group member a copy of the 'test' and a pen.

TEST

Instructions: Answer each question in order. If you are unable to answer any question, pass on to the next question and, if you have time, go back to the question. Read through all the questions before attempting the test.

1. Write your name in the top right-hand corner of the paper.

2. Print your address on the left-hand side of the paper.

3. Circle the correct answer:
   a. The tomato is a: vegetable, mineral, fruit?
   b. Paris is the capital of: Germany, France, Italy?
   c. Lira is the currency of: Austria, Belgium, Italy?

4. Raise your right hand to inform the group leader that you have completed the first three questions. When they nod you can continue with the test.

5. True or false? (tick the correct answer)
   a. Uranus is visible to the naked eye.   T/F
   b. The diameter of the moon is 3,476km.   T/F
   c. Antarctic means 'opposite' of the Arctic.   T/F

6. Is this word spelt correctly: 'Constantinople'. Yes/No

7. Stand up until the group leader tells you to sit down.

8. What is the opposite of 'Lethargy'?

9. What is the missing number from the following sequence: 5, 7, 11, 13, ? 17?

10. You should have read through the entire test paper before answering. Do not answer questions 1-9. Write your name at the top of the sheet and then remain quiet until the group leader declares the test over.

Worry

1

Equipment: pen and two small pieces of card for each member of the group

Give every member of the group a pen and piece of card. Ask them to think of some situations or phenomena which they find interesting or intriguing, such as: Why is the earth round? Why do we burp? Why don't cows fly? Why can't you eat loads of ice-cream without feeling sick? Ask each group member to write one question on their card which begins with the word 'why?'

Collect all the question cards and give out another card. On the second card the group should write an answer to their question. Each answer should begin with the word 'because'. Collect all the cards.

Shuffle and distribute all the 'why' cards and all the 'because' cards and ask each member to read their 'why' and 'because' cards, creating nonsense such as: 'Why do we burp? Because we'd explode!'

2

Equipment: small sheets of paper and a pen for each member of the group

Give each member of the group a piece of paper and a pen. Ask the group to agree on a definition for 'worry'.

- Is it being a wimp?
- Is it being stupid?
- Is it being too sensitive?
- Is it being realistic about your situation?

• Is it being frightened?

You might like to have a dictionary definition to give to the group after they have agreed on their definition.

Ask the group to write the agreed definition for 'worry' on the top of their piece of paper. Now ask them to write about one issue or concern that is 'worrying' them at the moment.

3

Equipment: balloons
flipchart

Give each group member a balloon. Ask each of them to inflate the balloon until it is approximately half-size; then stop the balloon from deflating by pinching the end of the balloon tight between fingers. Now, point to the first person on your left and ask them to name things that worry them. Draw a circle onto the flipchart and list the person's worries in the circle. Write that person's name below the circle. Ask the next person to name some of their worries and again draw a circle, write the worries in the centre and the person's name below the circle. Continue until every member of the group has contributed to the question.

Turn to the group and tell them to take a deep breath and blow up the balloon until they cannot blow any more. Repeat the exercise for every worry that they have named. This should cause a lot of giggles and result in some burst balloons!

Worship

Equipment: large sheet of paper with 'POWRISH' written in large letters
paper and pen for each person

Split the group into pairs and give each pair a piece of paper and a pen. Challenge them to make as many words as they can from the letters on the sheet. The winning pair can be awarded a clean paper tissue each.

Did any of the pairs manage to make the word 'worship' out of the letters? If not, rewrite the letters on the sheet to read 'WORSHIP'. Now ask the group to suggest definitions for the word 'worship'. What do they think it means? Try to agree a short sentence which the whole group are happy with as a definition of worship.